Are School UNIFORMS Good for Students?

By Katie Kawa

Published in 2018 by
KidHaven Publishing, an Imprint of Greenhaven Publishing, LLC
353 3rd Avenue
Suite 255
New York, NY 10010

Designer: Seth Hughes
Editor: Katie Kawa

Photo credits: Cover Floresco Productions/Cultura/Getty Images; p. 5 (top) sirtravelalot/ Shutterstock.com; pp. 5 (bottom), 13 © istockphoto.com/monkeybusinessimages; p. 7 (top-left) Karpova/Shutterstock.com; p. 7 (top-right) John Roman Images/Shutterstock.com; p. 7 (bottom-left) michaeljung/iStock/Thinkstock; p. 7 (bottom-right) Digital Vision./Photodisc/Thinkstock; p. 9 (top) DGLimages/iStock/Thinkstock; pp. 9 (bottom), 11, 21 (inset, left), 21 (inset, right) wavebreakmedia/ Shutterstock.com; p. 15 Wavebreakmedia/iStock/Thinkstock; p. 17 Iakov Filimonov/Shutterstock.com; p. 19 Klaus Vedfelt/Taxi/Getty Images; p. 21 (notepad) ESB Professional/Shutterstock.com; p. 21 (markers) Kucher Serhii/Shutterstock.com; p. 21 (photo frame) FARBAI/iStock/Thinkstock; p. 21 (inset, middle-left) monkeybusinessimages/iStock/Thinkstock; p. 21 (inset, middle-right) SerrNovik/ iStock/Thinkstock.

Cataloging-in-Publication Data

Names: Kawa, Katie.
Title: Are school uniforms good for students? / Katie Kawa.
Description: New York : KidHaven Publishing, 2018. | Series: Points of view | Includes index.
Identifiers: ISBN 9781534523401 (pbk.) | 9781534523425 (library bound) | ISBN 9781534523418 (6 pack) | ISBN 9781534523432 (ebook)
Subjects: LCSH: Students–Clothing–United States–Juvenile literature. | Students–United States– Uniforms–Juvenile literature. | Dress codes–United States–Juvenile literature.
Classification: LCC LB3024.K425 2018 | DDC 371.5′1–dc23

Printed in the United States of America

CPSIA compliance information: Batch #BS17KL: For further information contact Greenhaven Publishing LLC, New York, New York at 1-844-317-7404.

Please visit our website, www.greenhavenpublishing.com. For a free color catalog of all our high-quality books, call toll free 1-844-317-7404 or fax 1-844-317-7405.

CONTENTS

What Should Students WEAR?

What kinds of clothing do you wear to school? Some students can choose what they wear to school every day, and they can wear almost anything. Other students, however, don't have much of a choice. They wear uniforms, or a set kind of clothing worn by every student at their school.

Some people think schools should make students wear uniforms, while others think students should get to wear whatever they want. Knowing the reasons people have these points of view can help you decide how you feel about school uniforms.

Know the Facts!

By 2014, one in five public schools in the United States required students to wear uniforms.

Are school uniforms good for students? It's good to know all the facts so you can answer in an informed, or educated, way.

Who Wears A UNIFORM?

Students at all kinds of schools wear uniforms. However, uniforms are most commonly worn by students in private schools, including **religious** schools. These uniforms can include skirts or **jumpers**, certain kinds of pants or shorts, and shirts that must be a certain style or color. Some schools also require students to only wear certain kinds of socks and shoes.

Students aren't the only people who wear uniforms. Some jobs require people to wear uniforms. Police officers, nurses, firefighters, doctors, and airplane pilots are just some of the people who wear uniforms to work.

Know the Facts!

Some schools have a dress code instead of uniforms. A dress code is a set of rules for what people can wear. Dress codes generally give students more freedom than uniforms.

Uniforms are an important part of many jobs.

7

Fighting the Pressure to
FIT IN

Sometimes students tease each other because of the clothing they wear. People who wear certain brands or styles of clothing might get teased because they look different. Students might face **peer pressure** from their friends and classmates to dress a certain way to make friends.

People who support school uniforms believe this would happen less if students all had to dress the same. Uniforms can lower the chance that students will be bullied because of what they're wearing. This can be helpful for students who can't afford to wear the latest fashion trends.

Know the Facts!

According to one study, 90 percent of students in fourth through eighth grade have reported being bullied at school.

When students wear uniforms, they don't have to worry about wearing certain clothes to fit in.

Do Uniforms
REALLY HELP?

Although uniforms can help stop children from bullying each other because of the clothes they wear, they don't stop bullying completely. Bullies can single out students for how they choose to wear their uniform. For example, a girl might get teased for wearing a skirt instead of pants, even if both are part of her school's uniform.

Some people argue that uniforms can actually make young people the **targets** of bullies from other schools. Students who go to schools that don't require uniforms might bully students wearing uniforms because they're dressed differently.

Know the Facts!

Bullying that happens online or through text messages is called cyberbullying.

Students who wear uniforms can still be bullied because of how they look.

Following
THE RULES

Discipline, or the practice of following rules, is an important life skill. Rules are a part of everyday life—from the speed limits on the road to the rules in an office. Wearing a uniform at school gives children a rule to follow every day from the time they're young. This **encourages** discipline in schools.

Some people believe this sense of discipline helps students take their schoolwork more **seriously**. Uniforms make students look more **professional**. People who support school uniforms believe looking professional encourages students to act that way, too.

Know the Facts!

A study **published** in 2013 showed that within one year of requiring uniforms, multiple schools in Nevada reported that fighting and other discipline problems had decreased, or gone down.

Uniforms help even very young students learn to follow rules.

13

Less Diversity and
CREATIVITY

Although it's good for students to learn some discipline, people who oppose school uniforms believe there's such a thing as too much of it. They think school uniforms keep students from **expressing** themselves through their clothing. They want students to feel free to be themselves, which can't happen when they're being told what to wear.

Some people also believe school uniforms stop students from dressing in a way that honors different cultures, or ways of life, from around the world. By forcing students to dress the same, uniforms make classrooms a less **diverse** and creative place.

Know the Facts!

The first major study of the effect of uniforms on public schools was done in 1994 in Long Beach, California.

Young people often express themselves through the clothes they choose to wear. They can't do this when wearing a uniform.

Saving

MONEY

Buying clothes for school can be expensive. At the start of the school year, many families go back-to-school shopping, which often means buying many new clothes and spending a lot of money. Throughout the year, students often buy more clothes for each new season.

Wearing a uniform can lower the amount of money spent on clothing during a school year. People only need to buy a few pieces of clothing for a school uniform instead of many new outfits to keep up with what other students are wearing. This saves time and money.

Know the Facts!

In 2016, adults in the United States were expected to spend a total of $75.8 billion on back-to-school shopping. That amount includes money spent on clothing, shoes, and school supplies.

Many parents believe school uniforms help them save money on back-to-school shopping.

The Cost of
UNIFORMS

Although school uniforms might save families more money over time, they still cost money to buy. For families who are having trouble affording any kind of clothing, this can be hard.

If a school doesn't require a uniform, students can wear old clothing or clothing that can be bought for very little money. They can also buy small amounts of clothing throughout the year as needed. The basic parts of a uniform, however, must be bought all at once before a student can start school. This can be expensive.

Know the Facts!

As of 2013, the average cost of a school uniform was less than $150.

Some people donate, or give away, their children's old uniforms to families who have trouble paying for uniforms.

19

What's Your
POINT OF VIEW?

People have many other reasons for supporting and opposing school uniforms. Students often find uniforms to be uncomfortable. However, uniforms can help cut down on the amount of time students spend picking out clothes in the morning. This gives them more time to sleep or eat a healthy breakfast.

After seeing the arguments for and against school uniforms, how do you feel about them? Are they good for students? Remember to think about all the facts you've learned before forming your point of view.

Know the Facts!

Uniforms were more common in city schools than in schools in other areas as of 2013, which was the year the most recent study on school uniforms was done.

Are SCHOOL UNIFORMS good for STUDENTS?

YES

- Students aren't bullied as much for their clothing and feel less peer pressure to dress a certain way.

- Uniforms encourage students to be disciplined.

- Parents spend less money on uniforms than they do on other clothing throughout the year.

- Students who wear uniforms take less time getting ready in the morning.

NO

- Uniforms don't stop bullying completely and might even lead to bullying between children from different schools.

- Uniforms take away students' freedom of expression and make for less diverse classrooms.

- Uniforms can cost a lot of money all at once.

- Uniforms are sometimes uncomfortable to wear.

This chart can help you form an educated point of view about school uniforms.

21

GLOSSARY

diverse: Made up of many qualities that are different from one another.

encourage: To try to get someone to do something.

express: To show a person's true self or creative abilities.

jumper: A sleeveless dress often worn with a shirt under it.

peer pressure: A feeling that one must do the same things as others to be liked by them.

professional: Done as if for a job, with great care.

publish: To print something so it can be seen by the public.

religious: Relating to a system of beliefs, often belief in God, held with faith and strong feeling.

seriously: Done with much thought or work.

target: A person someone aims an attack at.

For More
INFORMATION

WEBSITES

"School Uniforms" Survey Results

teacher.scholastic.com/kidusasu/uniforms/chart1.htm
This website features a graph showing percentages of students who support and oppose school uniforms grouped by where they live, as well as questions about the graph.

StopBullying.gov—Kids

www.stopbullying.gov/kids/
This website provides information about what to do if you or someone you know is being bullied for reasons that might include the clothing they wear to school.

BOOKS

Carole, Bonnie. *School Uniforms, Yes or No.* Vero Beach, FL: Rourke Educational Media, 2016.

Fortuna, Lois. *Getting Ready for School.* New York, NY: Gareth Stevens Publishing, 2016.

INDEX